AMAZING ACTIVITIES FOR FANS OF MARIO KART TOUR

WORD SEARCHES, CROSSWORD PUZZLES, DOT TO DOT, MAZES, AND BRAIN TEASERS TO IMPROVE YOUR SKILLS

Brian Boone

SKY PONY PRESS

NEW YORK

CORE CAST CROSSWORD

The answers in this puzzle are all the names of the biggest, most popular, and most famous drivers in *Mario Kart Tour*.

ACROSS

6. Mario's brother
7. Skeleton dragon
9. Flowery
11. Waluigi's accomplice
12. A real "fun guy"
14. Dinosaur
15. A real "shell guy"

DOWN

1. She can carry a tune
2. Wario's accomplice
3. Think flight and eggs
4. A lady mushroom
5. Royal racer
8. Sounds like a flower
10. Luigi's brother
13. Also known as King Koopa

NOT THE RIGHT KART

Look at all these standard racing karts. They're all the same except one. Can you find which one is unlike the rest?

1

2

3

4

5

6

7

8

PLACE THE PLACEMENTS

Based on the clues below, can you fill out the chart with which character finished in what place in the Luigi's Mansion race?

1. Mario finished the race three spots before Daisy.

2. Toadette's spot is double the number of Daisy's position.

3. Luigi did three spots better than Toadette, but three spots worse than Wario.

4. Wario did three times better than Koopa Troopa.

5. Bowser finished just behind Koopa Troopa.

6. Donkey Kong finished somewhere in the top 3.

BOWSER	LUIGI	DONKEY KONG	MARIO
WARIO	KOOPA TROOPA	TOADETTE	DAISY

A RACE AROUND THE BLOCKS

Make your way through this extremely twisty *Mario Kart Tour* race, but avoid those dreaded, explosive item blocks. Be sure to choose the right entrance!

KART SEARCH

Find the names of all the karts in the puzzle below.

Pipe Frame

Birthday Girl

Mushmellow

Koopa Dasher

Bullet Basher

Mach Eight

Daytripper

Turbo Yoshi

Soda Jet

Super Blooper

Gold Blooper

Flame Flyer

Barrel Train

B Dasher

Yellow Taxi

Badwagon

```
I B Q K T D M R T M J R Y T N K J D M M
L A Z W U L E Q A F A E E C K Q L R F M
R T Z R W H P C G R D L H L R O N P V E V
T E N N S Z H X E G I S L A O P X Z W G
P Y Y A E C P S W H A O W P M E G G Q
U E D L I B P K W O S B W X A S U J B P
K B X G F I E J C Q O T T J D S D R Z B
Z X H I R E D Y S A Y E A F A B I G R S
I T Q T B G M Z E W O L X W S K B G U R
E L Y K I U Y A I S B L I E H N B P E B
H A L X Y F W E L M R U B C E N E P A E
D P K U G P T X H F U B G W R R O R M N
U G V Z B A B D C P T N G L B O R A O T
D S Q P Q H W M S J B X S L L E R G E O
B I R T H D A Y G I R L O B L F A J Y A
M G B K D Z G A A I G O D T E W A W F Z
M U S H M E L L O W P L R P D D U D B V
Q T W P E Y D O B E O A I A O A W R E S
B Q V J P P E T R G I P B S K V A U N S
S X Z D H F N U Z N F M F Z T M O G D R
```

CONNECT THE DOTS: LOOKS GOOD

Connect the dots to find the accessory that Birdo never races without.

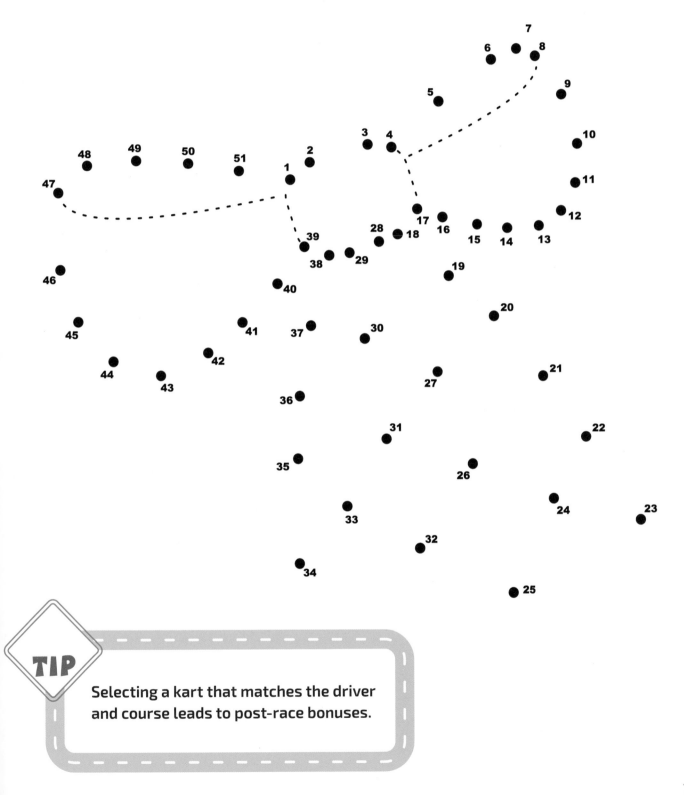

Selecting a kart that matches the driver and course leads to post-race bonuses.

LUCKY HIDDEN WORD

There's a very rare and special item in *Mario Kart Tour* that gives a racer a whole slew of items all at once. In the crossword below, enter in the names of those items (and the name of the block that gives them). Down the middle, another word will be revealed — the name of one more special item.

1. Fruit

2. Koopa's back

3. Explosive

4. Fungus

5. Sounds like trouble

6. What the whole bountiful block is called

7. Targeted and hard to crack

ANSWER

SQUARED UP: ITEMS BY PICTURE

The red shell, Yoshi egg, Piranha Plant, and coin blocks can each appear just once in each row, each column, and each of the four smaller boxes. Draw or write in the remaining empty boxes with the names or pictures of each racing reward.

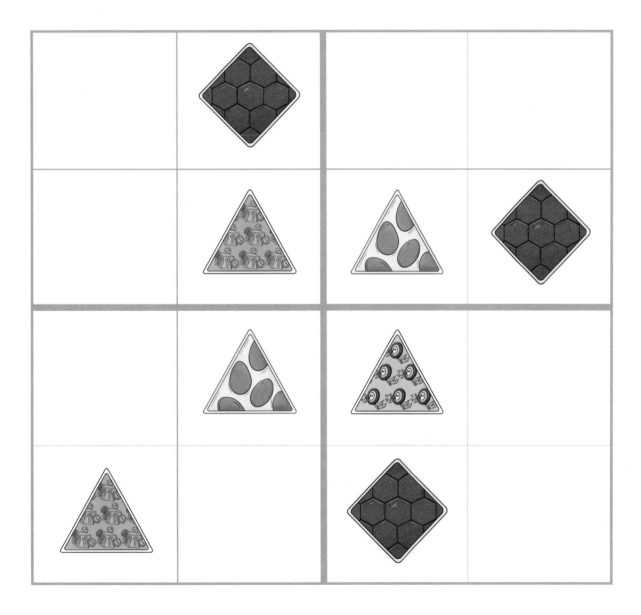

RACE TO THE BOTTOM

Start at the dot below each character and work your way down the ladders to find out which character finished the race in what order. One thing: Every time you move down to a horizontal (sideways) line, you have to take it over to the next vertical (up and down) and continue.

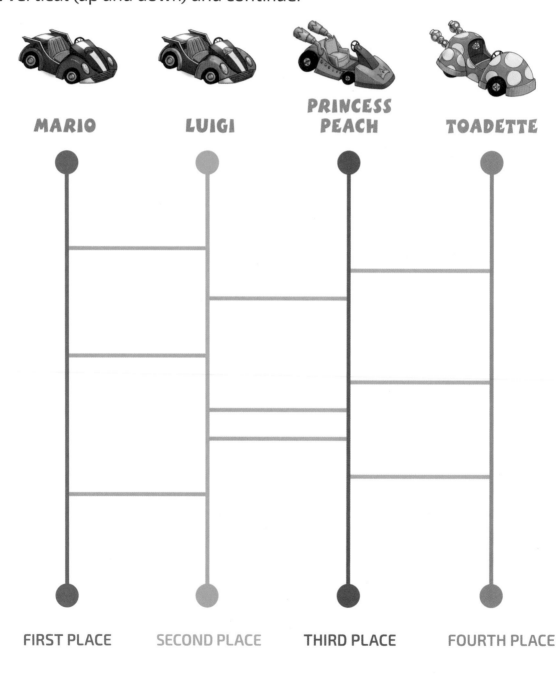

MARIO **LUIGI** **PRINCESS PEACH** **TOADETTE**

FIRST PLACE   SECOND PLACE   THIRD PLACE   FOURTH PLACE

_____   _____   _____   _____

FIND THE LUCKY 7

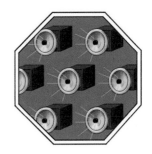

Nailing a "Lucky 7" block — packed with seven racing rewards instead of only one — can really make your whole tour. Can you figure out which one of these blocks holds the "Lucky 7" inside?

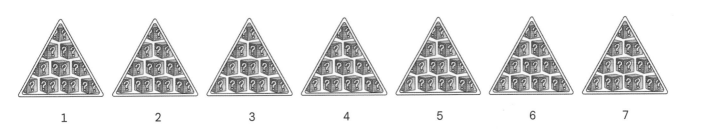

1   2   3   4   5   6   7

CLUES

1. It's not on the far left.

2. It's surrounded by at least two other blocks on both sides.

3. Starting from the one on the far left, it's not an oddly-numbered block.

4. It's not on the far right.

ANSWER _____

TIP

Dinosaurs only look dangerous. Run into a dino's head in Dino Dino Jungle for a quick speed boost.

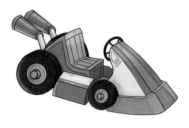

BIG BEN, LITTLE DIFFERENCES

Mario Kart Tour features a race through London, home of the famous tower featuring the giant clock known as Big Ben. Can you spot 5 differences between these two clock towers?

WORDS ARE FALLING

Fill in the grid with the letters listed below — in exact up-and-down order, into the columns directly above. You'll spell out a unique feature distinct to *Mario Kart Tour*, not found in other *Mario Kart* games.

```
            E       E       Y

    H   R   V   C   R   E               I   N

C   M   A   R   A   O   T   K   R   R   T

T   O   A   R   I   H   A   S   A   T   O

B   E   U   U   N   L   O   C   K   E   D
```

BEFORE, AFTER, AND IN-BETWEEN

The answers (the names of some Bonus Challenges) will be revealed by adding letters to the empty boxes that come before, between, or after the letters placed directly below the boxes. (If you get to a Z, start over again with A.) We gave you the first one.

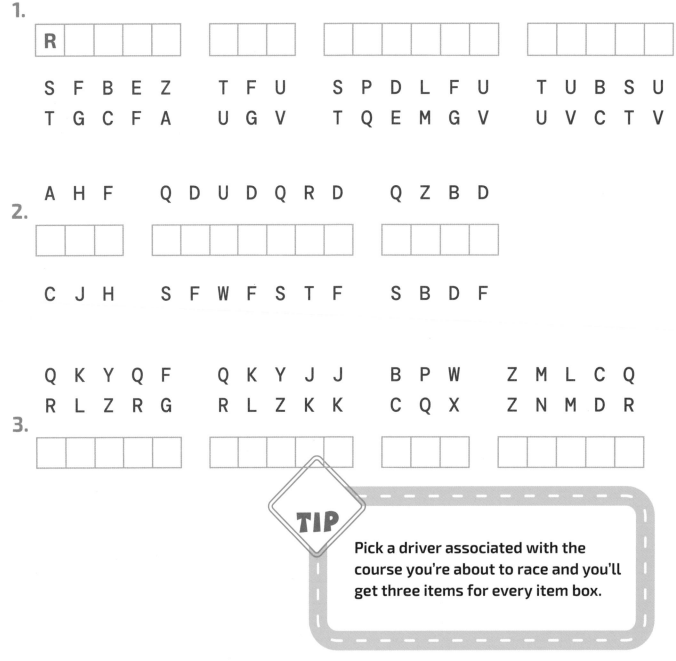

1.

| R | | | | |

S F B E Z
T G C F A

T F U
U G V

S P D L F U
T Q E M G V

T U B S U
U V C T V

2.

A H F
Q D U D Q R D
Q Z B D

| | | |

| | | | | | |

| | | |

C J H
S F W F S T F
S B D F

Q K Y Q F
R L Z R G

Q K Y J J
R L Z K K

B P W
C Q X

Z M L C Q
Z N M D R

3.

| | | | | |

| | | | | |

| | | |

| | | | |

TIP

Pick a driver associated with the course you're about to race and you'll get three items for every item box.

COVERING YOUR TRACKS

For this crossword puzzle, use the clues to find out the names of different courses and tracks in *Mario Kart Tour*.

ACROSS

3. A prehistoric trip
4. Very colorful
6. Original character, basic race track
9. Shop 'til you drop
11. A royal trip
12. Like what people played before video games
13. The big house
14. A tasty treat

DOWN

1. Think dry
2. There's "mushroom" to win
5. Sun and sand
7. Monkeying around
8. Birds and beaches
10. A rocky pursuit

FIND THE DIFFERENT DRIVERS

There are drivers in *Mario Kart Tour*, and then different, special, unlockable versions of those drivers. Can you find them in the grid below?

Vacation
Ice Mario
Musician
Kimono
Hakama
Santa
Happi
Penguin
Cherub
Detective
Pastry Chef
Bus Driver
Hiker
Aurora
Wintertime
Party Time

```
X H D U T R A G V V F Q X X C Z W E O E
H B G Q I U M J V D H N W C K I D R H M
Y A B A R K Y Z X A H A X U N N E E S U
M X P O O Q Z J E M C H G T D O T K X B
C D R P B A E M C V F A E L E I E I P W
A A I C B I Z K N K R T L U C C H F J
H F Q B M T B C D C T O W I U V T Z L M
N Q Q U Y L W G N I E I S V O H I W S B
E K K T E O Q A M H Z R F J I N D V D K
D K R Y N O I E A H Z A W G D T E Y C O
P A Z O Z C C K L X V M C H E R U B Z R
P A M O I X A U A J O E Z R A P D X C F
I I S S D M G T L P W C T B M E Y J V T
K U U T A G N H N N I I Q W K N Z X P S
V M G E R A N Z J D X K P J O G L U F H
W R C D S Y B U S D R I V E R U Z N C M
Y Y K O L V C W A Q W I C E A I R S S L
K W O K K K K H T A Y Q J F F N R G D F
N F X G V N P E W J M Y A Q Q R K C R
Q S R P D L Z J B F G F E J L G G V F W
```

THE RACE IS ON!

Make your way through the *Mario Kart Tour* race. Which player is likely to reach the finish line the fastest?

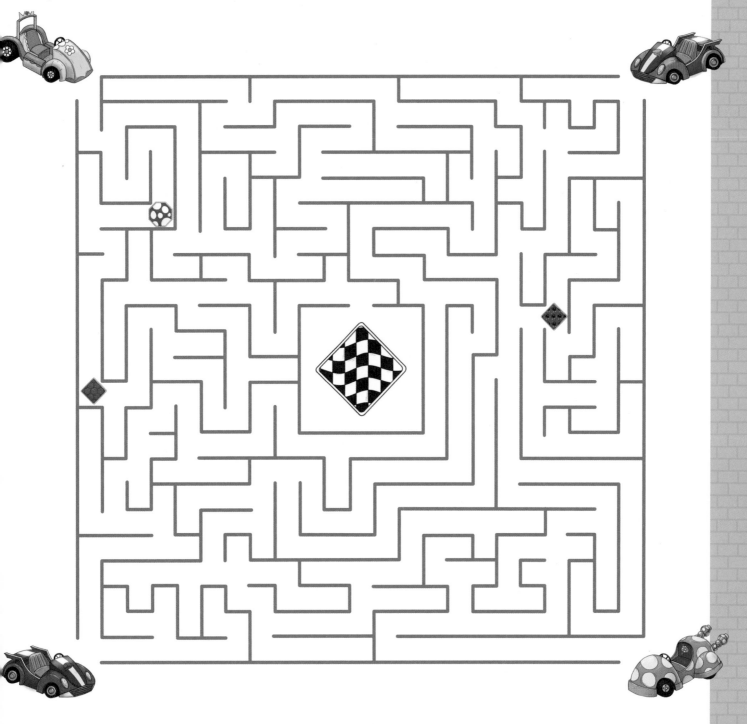

JUST TWO WORDS

Identify each of the following by two-word clues. The first letter of each word will spell out the name of one of the quirkiest tracks in *Mario Kart Tour*.

1. Evil Mario

2. Hot floats

3. Cloud sitter

4. Drifting charge

5. Tallest Koopaling

6. Mushroom guy

7. Cold bloomer

8. Female singer

9. Redeem? Prize!

10. Dragon track

11. Little princess

12. Mobile fruit

13. Boat kart

14. British racetrack

ANSWER

READ AROUND

Start at the green flag. Write every third letter on the spaces until all have been used. If you place them correctly, you'll reveal a benefit of losing. Remember to cross out the letters as you go.

E				

| | | | | | .
|---|---|---|---|---|

PICTURE CROSSWORD

Place the pictures into the crossword. Okay, that doesn't make sense. Take the name of the common *Mario Kart Tour* element pictured, and then find where it goes in the crossword.

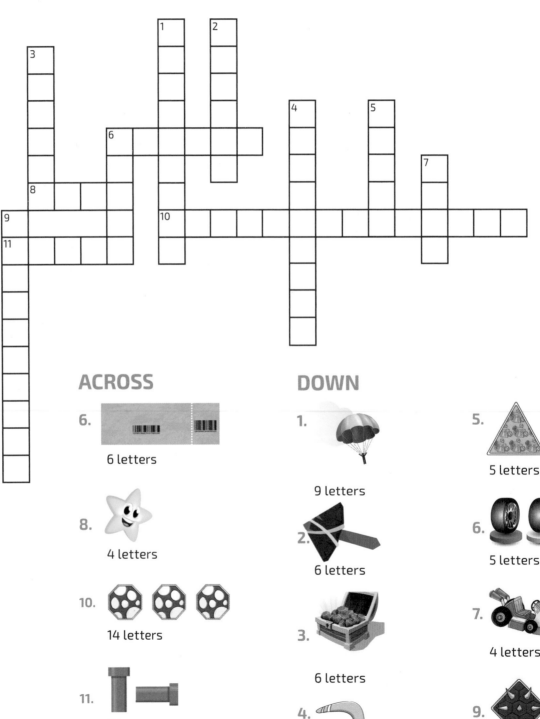

ACROSS

6. 6 letters

8. 4 letters

10. 14 letters

11. 5 letters

DOWN

1.
9 letters

2. 6 letters

3. 6 letters

4.
9 letters

5. 5 letters

6. 5 letters

7.
4 letters

9.
10 letters

UNSCRAMBLE IT!

Rearrange each of the following words. Then, take the letters in each entry's red box and unscramble that word — which will reveal the name of a valuable racing tool.

1. HYYGUS

2. KUATLI

3. HIYOS

4. DLGUIW

5. EOSRNBDY

6. ORY

ANSWER

___ ___ ___ ___ ___ ___

CONNECT THE DOTS: FIRE AWAY!

Connect the dots to find the one place in *Mario Kart Tour* that is more full of prizes than any item block.

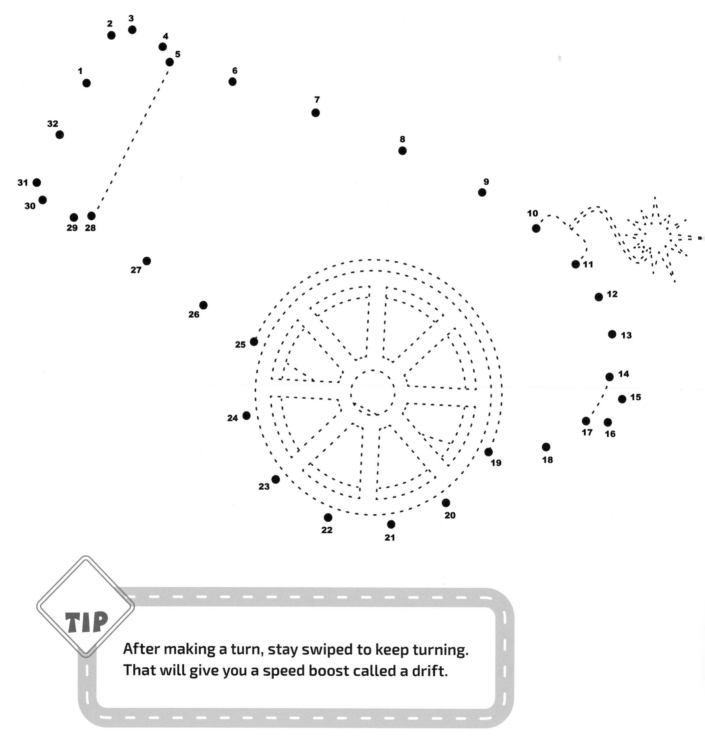

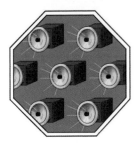

YOU CAN DRAW IT: KART!

Use the grid to copy the picture one square at a time. Examine the lines in each small square in the top grid, and then re-create those lines in the corresponding square in the bottom grid.

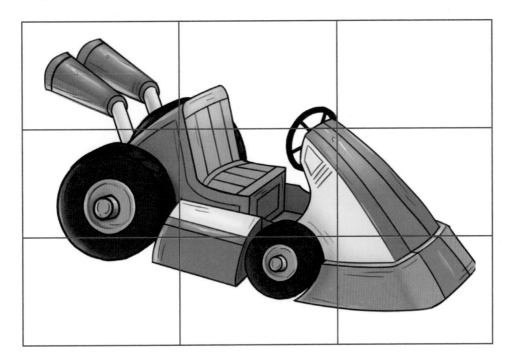

SQUARED UP: KOOPALINGS

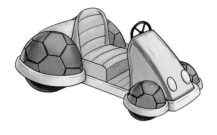

The names of the Koopa kids (plus one family friend) can appear just once in each row, each column, and each of the nine smaller boxes. Fill in the remaining empty boxes with the initials to represent each character.

IGGY	I		**BOWSER**	B
MORTON	M		**LUDWIG**	G
WENDY	W		LEMMY	E
ROY	R		**DRY BOWSER**	D
LARRY	Y			

R	E		I			D		B
D				M	B	W		
M				W			E	I
				W		I		Y
	D	B			Y			
Y	W			R			B	
	D	G			R			
	I					M	G	
	R	Y				B		

SPELLING TEST

How well do you know your *Mario Kart* spelling? In each *Mario Kart Tour* item below, there's one right letter replaced with one wrong letter. Find the wrong letter in each word, and then put the incorrect letters together to form the name of a kart outfitted with Mini-Turbo Plus.

1. **BOWZER** _____

2. **VANCOUVUR** _____

3. **MUCHMELLOW** _____

4. **CALIMARI DESERT** _____

5. **SHOOPER** _____

6. **DROPLIT** _____

7. **NORTON** _____

8. **DASHIR II** _____

ANSWER

___ ___ ___ ___ ___ ___ ___ ___

FIND THAT BONUS

In the puzzle below are the words listed in the column — all of which are bonuses you'd be very happy to accept in a game of *Mario Kart Tour.*

Green Shell

Coin

Spiny Shell

Lightning

Super Horn

Blooper

Mega Mushroom

Bob-omb

Red Shell

Fire Flower

Heart

Yoshi Egg

Bowser Shell

Triple Mushroom

Boomerang Flower

Star

Bullet Bill

Boo

```
R R G B G K B D N F F M I S M
F E C N O R B M I A O P Y P O
U D W Z I O E R O O W O O I O
T S R O E N E E R B S V N N R
R H Q D L F T H N H O X S Y H
A E Z L L F S H I S Y B E S S
E L U O K U G E G E H C F H U
H L W N M W G N B I B E P E M
B E I A M G V M A A L Y L L E
R O G Y B O W S E R S H E L L
C E C Q U H O F T Y E J P I P
M L L I B T E L L U B M H I I
C X G J L W Y Y U T N N O K R
S U P E R H O R N S T A R O T
R E P O O L B G F G F W O E B
```

TIP

You can get even more coins in Gold Rush if you play as Gold Mario, who attracts coins like a magnet!

READ AROUND

Start at the green flag. Write every third letter on the spaces until all have been used. If you place them correctly, you'll reveal a *Mario Kart Tour* racing tip. Remember to cross out the letters as you go.

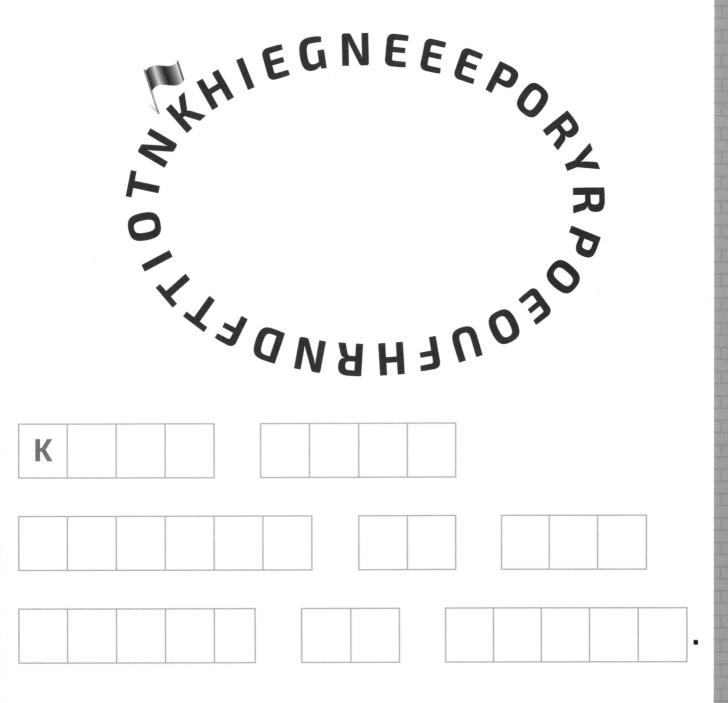

SAME LETTER CONNECTOR

Boxes connected by lines contain the same letter. We've given you some letters, which you can use to fill in some boxes. Others you'll have to figure out on your own. Once all the boxes are filled in, you'll find a hint about what happens in frenzy mode.

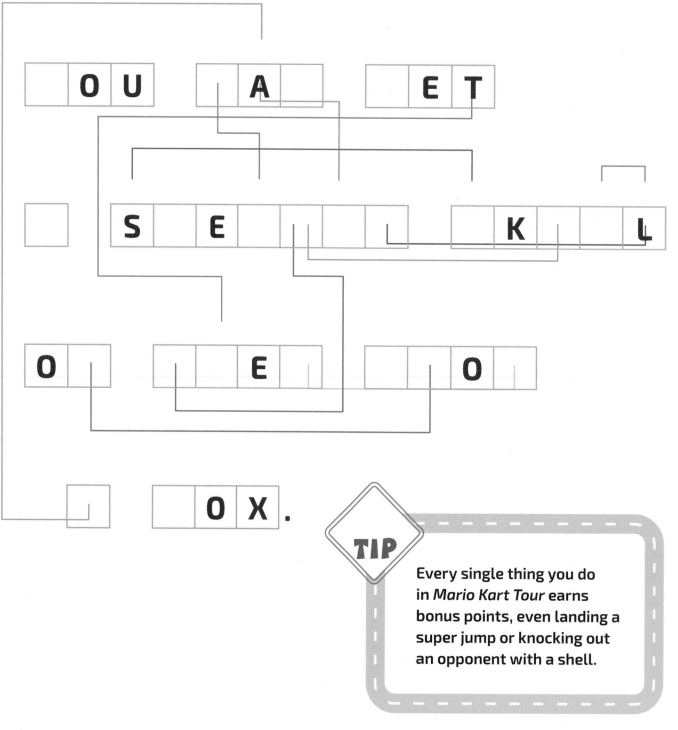

TIP

Every single thing you do in *Mario Kart Tour* earns bonus points, even landing a super jump or knocking out an opponent with a shell.

REARRANGE AND ADD

Take the name of a *Mario Kart Tour* character from column A and find the word in column B that's made up of all the same letters as that name . . . plus one extra letter. Then, take the extra letters, unscramble them, and you'll find out what Toadette makes whenever she wins a race.

COLUMN A	COLUMN B	
DAISY	CHAPEL	_____
PEACH	YAWNED	_____
WENDY	RARELY	_____
ROY	DISMAY	_____
LARRY	MONITOR	_____
MORTON	ROSY	_____

ANSWER

_____ _____ _____ _____ _____ _____

A RACE FOR THREE

This maze is a race to the finish for Mario, Luigi, and Princess Peach. They all enter the race, but only one has chosen the right path. Who is it?

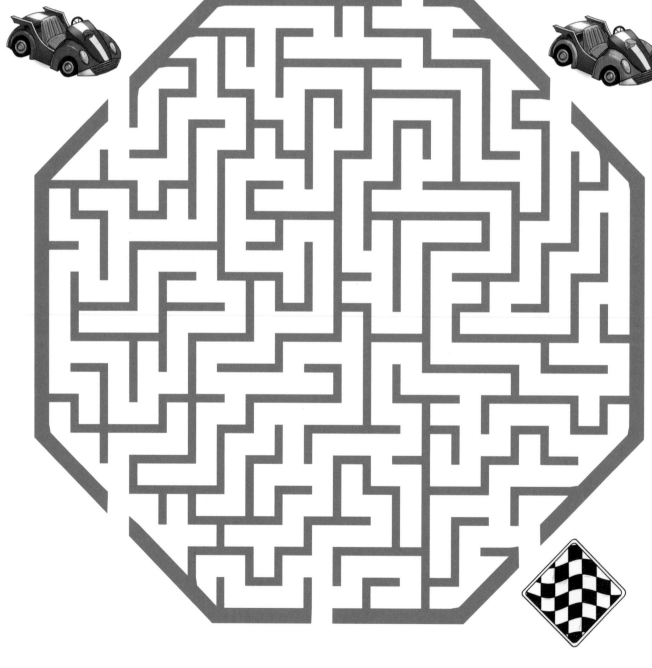

HAZARDS CROSSWORD

The answers to these crossword clues are all things you'd find on a *Mario Kart Tour* track (and should probably avoid).

ACROSS

5. Worse than a regular jar
6. Giant Yoshi?
7. Pinball tool
8. Its name sounds like the sound it makes
11. It means to fly low
12. Ah, shoot!
13. Volcanic
14. _____ sticker
15. Rhymes with great

DOWN

1. Full of monkeys
2. Get back to the farm!
3. Choo-choo-choose correctly
4. Feels clammy
5. They step to the side
9. So slippery
10. Did it just rain?
12. Moving mushroom

REAL OR FAKE TRACKS?

There are a lot of colorfully named tracks in *Mario Kart Tour*. Can you identify which ones are real, and which ones are not?

REAL	FAKE	
☐	○	**Hollywood Shuffle**
☐	○	**New York Minute**
☐	○	**Toronto Turnpike**
☐	○	**Vancouver Velocity**
☐	○	**Cake Mountain**
☐	○	**Choco Island**
☐	○	**Spooky Plains**
☐	○	**Ghost Valley**
☐	○	**Strawberry Island**
☐	○	**Vanilla Lake**
☐	○	**Wario Foosball**
☐	○	**Waluigi Pinball**
☐	○	**Dessert Desert**
☐	○	**Frappe Snowland**
☐	○	**Happy Village**
☐	○	**Daisy Hills**
☐	○	**Kong Kong Island**
☐	○	**Rock Rock Mountain**
☐	○	**Boo Gardens**
☐	○	**Dino Dino Jungle**

TIP

Not planning on playing today? Log in anyway — you can earn coin bonuses just for checking in.

A PUZZLE TO FLY THROUGH

Find the names of gliders and other flying accessories in *Mario Kart Tour*.

Boomerang Brothers

Parafoil

Le Tricolore

Strawberry Crepe

Super Glider

Parachute

Droplet

Paper

Piston

Piranha Plant

Peach Parasol

Lightning

Pink Flower

Oilpaper

Shell

Wario Wing

Plaid Ribbon

Swooper

Heart Balloons

Fireworks

```
C G X S N G P N O G B F A R V U Y V A U
N Q E V D U I O W N O N A E M B F F H R
R E P A P T N B P I O U W D E N T B D N
I E H N L E K B B N M B P I C F N I Y L
P B O L R L F I Y T E D I L N E A C O E
U A E U F P L R T H R Z D G X V L L V T
V H R F B O O D B G A A D R A C P H M R
S Y A A Z R W I L I N W C E R Y A W B I
D R O P C D E A A L G A V P W P H J X C
R O Q C M H R L A V B R T U U N N I O O
U O I J F B U P A E R I O S L T A W E L
R E P O O W S T B E O O A I M F R U E O
P A R A F O I L E N T W V A L O I G L R
S K R O W E R I F F H I D D U P P E I E
U M J L Q Q F A R I E N X A U H A U A B
R A F A O Q D I U N R G N Z Q C X P V L
X D O G S K V F T P S O N I K S M L E J
S T R A W B E R R Y C R E P E C T X R R
L Y N J B O S H E A R T B A L L O O N S
P E A C H P A R A S O L P I S T O N U B
```

33

SQUARED UP: ITEMS BY PICTURE

The Bullet Bill, Coin Box, Piranha Plant, Red Shell, Mushroom, and Bob-omb can appear only once in each row, column, and box. Can you find the right spot for each familiar *Mario Kart* symbol and place them there?

TOWER OF POWER

The famous Eiffel Tower pops up in the Paris Promenade race in *Mario Kart Tour*. Nine of them appear below, but only two are the same. Can you identify the twins?

1

2

3

4

5

6

7

8

9

SO MANY MARIOS

Each word below is a different variation of Mario found in *Mario Kart Tour*. Unscramble each, and use the letters in the numbered square to reveal a familiar character.

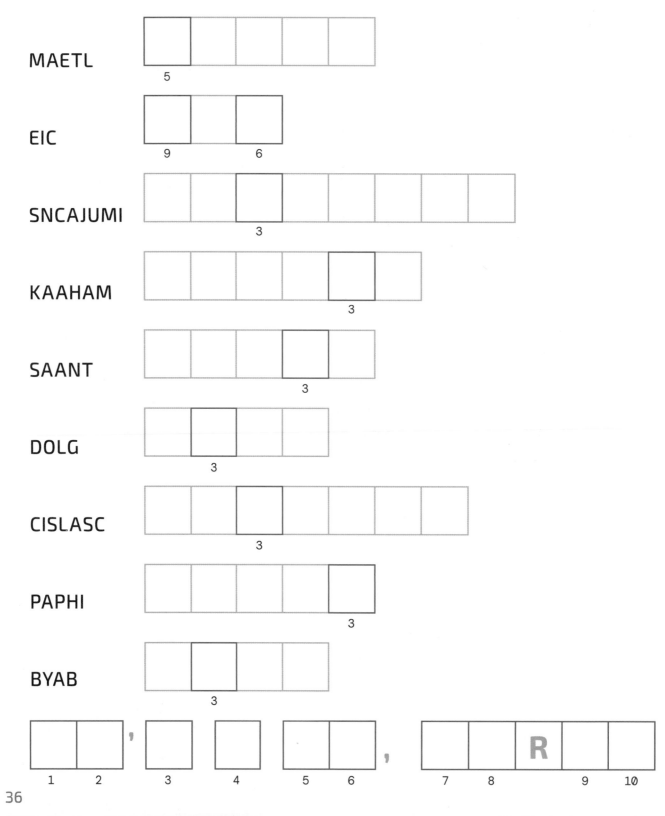

MAETL

EIC

SNCAJUMI

KAAHAM

SAANT

DOLG

CISLASC

PAPHI

BYAB

PLACE THE PLACEMENTS

Based on the clues below, can you fill out the chart with which character finished in what place in the Frappe Snowland race?

SHY GUY	DRY BONES	PEACH	TOAD
PAULINE	LARRY	LUDWIG	KING BOO

1. Larry finished five spots above his brother.

2. King Boo placed in the top 3, but he didn't win the race.

3. Toad placed three spots below King Boo.

4. A female racer won the race, but it's not Pauline.

5. Pauline's position is half the number of Shy Guy's.

6. Dry Bones edged out Toad.

READ AROUND

Start at the green flag. Write every third letter on the spaces until all have been used. If you place them correctly, you'll reveal a *Mario Kart Tour* tip. Remember to cross out the letters as you go.

WORD LADDER

Can you transform the word "TOAD" into "KART" in just six steps, changing only one letter each time? Answer the clues, and you'll get to the finish line.

TOAD

_____ 1. Rainbow

_____ 2. Primal scream

_____ 3. Wild pig

_____ 4. Like a kart for the water

_____ 5. Anagram of brat

KART

TIP

Loading the game devours a ton of phone battery. Just before you enter the game, turn on the phone's power-saving option to ensure no race interruptions.

TAKE ON KONG!

It's you versus Donkey Kong and Diddy Kong! Follow the paths for each kart and figure out who wins the race!

WORDS ARE FALLING

Fill in the grid with the letters listed below — in exact up-and-down order — into the columns directly above. You'll spell out a unique feature distinct to *Mario Kart Tour*, not found in other *Mario Kart* games.

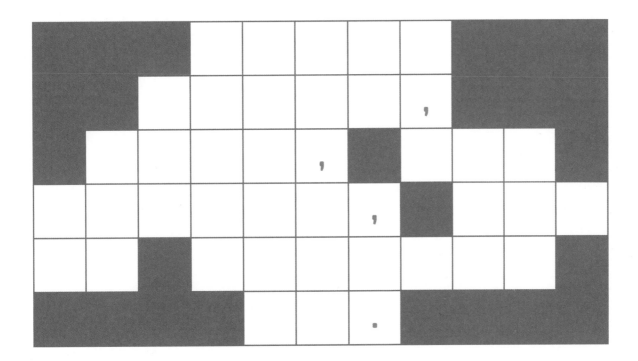

```
            V
      E  C  E
      A  T  E
   K  R  R  E  R  R  Y  N  D
G  L  A  D  E  V  R  A  C  A
B  E  I  L  U  P  E  L  E  D  N
```

DRIVEN OUT OF THE REAL WORLD

Place the words in the crossword. All of them related to *Mario Kart Tour* tracks based on real life things.

ACROSS

1. France
3. Sandy
6. "The City That Never Sleeps"
8. A big house
9. Bigger than a town
11. Smaller than mountains
12. It's British
13. A tropical forest

DOWN

1. An old-fashioned video game
2. Water near a beach
4. Capital of Japan
5. Taller than a hill
7. North of the U.S.
10. Surrounded by water

FUN-NAMED KART WORD SEARCH

The exclusive gold pass karts aren't only powerful, they've got some killer names. Find their names in the puzzle below.

Black Circuit
Radish Rider
Swift Jack
Quickshaw
Kabuki Dasher
Trickster
Ghost Ride
Carrot Kart
Cheermellow
Wildfire Flyer
Ribbon Rider
Double Decker
Jingle Bells
Macharon
Platinum Taxi
Glam Bruiser
Gilded Prancer
Apple Kart
Comet Tail

```
Y R R K C G M U U W A M R A R X S N A W
U E E N A E F P B C O Z A E W L O S P T
P Y D B R B G D J R S L C C L A W J R G
V L I O R H U B Y V W N L E H I M A H H
J F R K O L D K G Z A L B E F A K H H K
V E N I T U I A I R B E P T M E R C F Y
Q R O L K B A A P D L L J W L R H O D L
M I B B A F G D B G A A Q P U Z E U N C
D F B W R S E E N T C S P J Z R L E I W
O D I Y T D B I I K I A H U T I V P H O
U L R O L L J N V T J B D E N A I X X C
B I J I J R U B Z R S I S E R M O N G E
L W G X M M E N G L A M B R U I S E R D
E M Z I T T K T L W A H S K C I U Q J I
D W B A Y V U G S R E D I R H S I D A R
E M X A B M F V U K C O M E T T A I L T
C I W H C R M D X L C U V C L W B I L S
K B L A C K C I R C U I T D Y Y C A B O
E S U Y K P S A Y U T B R P R W T R H H
R P A P Q U Y O X R L Y D T Z T O Y R G
```

JUST TWO WORDS

Identify each of the following by two-word clues. The first letter of each word will spell out the name of one of the most unique characters in *Mario Kart Tour*.

1. Smiling turtle _____

2. Cold plant _____

3. "Minute" race _____

4. Shiny guy _____

5. Spiny dad _____

6. Purple umbrella _____

7. Tough tire _____

ANSWER _____

TIP

Get a big speed boost right out of the starting gate. When the countdown timer hits "2," hold your finger down on the phone to accelerate . . . and then blast off!

WORD LADDER

Can you transform the word "KART" into "FIRE" in just 10 steps, changing only one letter each time? Answer the clues, and you'll get to the finish line.

KART

_____ 1. Section

_____ 2. Not the future

_____ 3. DK _____

_____ 4. Low guitar

_____ 5. Bowser is one

_____ 6. On Mario's foot

_____ 7. 12 inches

_____ 8. A treehouse

_____ 9. Golf word

FIRE

SQUARED UP: TOUR STOPS

Each of these nine *Mario Kart Tour* spots can appear just once in each row, each column, and each of the nine smaller boxes. Fill in the remaining empty boxes with the initials to represent each locale.

NEW YORK N	**HALLOWEEN** H	
TOKYO T	**ICE** I	
PARIS P	**WINTER** W	
LONDON L	**MARIO BROS.** M	
VANCOUVER V		

N					T		I	
	T		V	H		P		
	L	M				N		T
	W		M				T	
T		N	H	I				
H				L			V	W
	H		V			T		
P	T		W					L
				P			W	H

BEFORE, AFTER, AND IN-BETWEEN

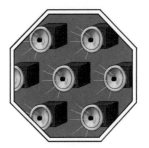

The answers (the names of some Bonus Challenges) will be revealed by adding letters to the empty boxes that come before, between, or after the letters placed directly below the boxes. (If you get to a Z, start over again with A.) We gave you the first one.

1.

| G | | | | | | | | | | | | | | | |

H P   P N   C B   U B L F E P X O
I   Q Q O D C   V C M G F Q Y P

2.

F K H C D Q   B H Z K K D M F D

| | | | | | | | | | | | | | | | |

H M J E F S   D I B M M F O H F

Q R C C P   A J C Y P   M D   M Z Q R Y A J C Q
R S D D Q   B K D Z Q   N E   N A R S Z B K D R

3.

| | | | | | | | | | | | | | | | | | | | | | |

TIP

You'll earn more EXP if you race a bunch of courses, not going back and re-playing ones you've already done.

READ AROUND

Read around this puzzle to reveal a way to get big prizes in *Mario Kart Tour*. The first letter is at the green flag and has been done for you. Write every third letter from there on the spaces below. Remember to cross out the letters as you go.

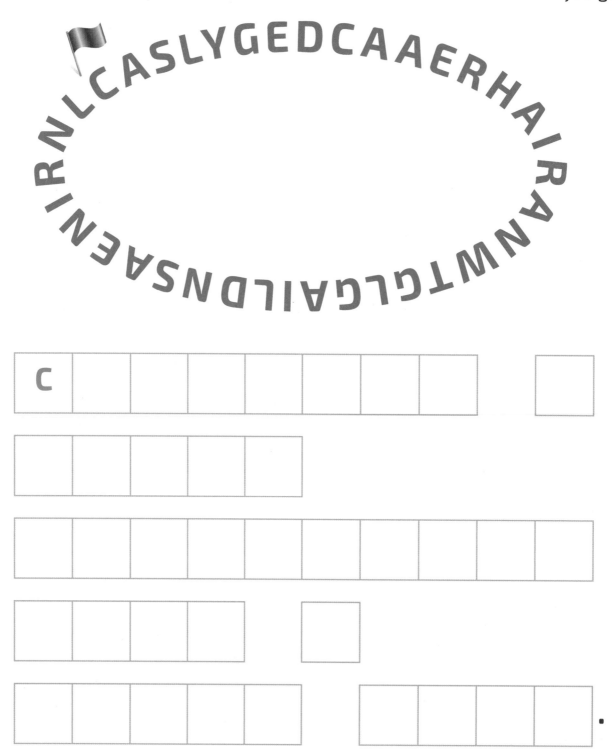

CASLYGEDCAAERHAIR

ANWTGLGAILDNSAENIRNL

| C | | | | | | | | | | | |

| | | | | | |

| | | | | | | | | | | |

| | | | | | | |

| | | | | | | | | | | .

MARIO MATH

With all the coins in *Mario Kart Tour*, a lot of money changes hands. In these puzzles below, determine if you've got enough cash for various power-ups and upgrades.

◎ **ITEM TICKET**	50	◎ **POINT BOOST TICKET**	100
◎ **NORMAL KART OR GLIDER**	500	◎ **QUICK TICKET**	1,000
◎ **NORMAL DRIVER**	800	◎ **SUPER KART OR GLIDER**	2,000
◎ **SUPER DRIVER**	3,000	◎ **HIGH-END KART OR GLIDER**	10,000
◎ **HIGH-END DRIVER**	12,000		

1. In a single race, the number of coins that can be earned is 99. How many single races would you have to race to get the maximum number of coins in to buy a new normal-level kart?

   _____

2. A coin rush can yield 300 coins. With just coins (no ruby-triggered multipliers), how many coin rushes, worth of coins would you need to upgrade to a super driver?

   _____

3. Let's say you have 400 coins saved up. How many item tickets could you buy with that?

   _____

4. How many coins would you need to upgrade to a high-end driver, kart, and glider all at once?

   _____

5. Which would cost more coins? Buying 3 normal drivers or a super kart plus 2 point boost tickets?

   _____

6. If you earned 300 coins in a coin rush every day of the month of October, how many coins would that give you?

   _____

7. How many super drivers would that buy, and how many quick tickets could you buy with what's leftover?

   _____

CONNECT THE DOTS: FLOATING FRENZY

Connect the dots to find the portable home of a familiar *Mario Kart Tour* driver.

TIP

Short on money to buy stuff in the Tour shop? Spend a few rubies and play Gold Rush to earn some cash.

ITEM RACE

Start at the dot below each character's name and work your way down the ladders to determine which character gets what item. One thing: Every time you move down to a horizontal (sideways) line, you have to take it over to the next vertical (up and down) and continue.

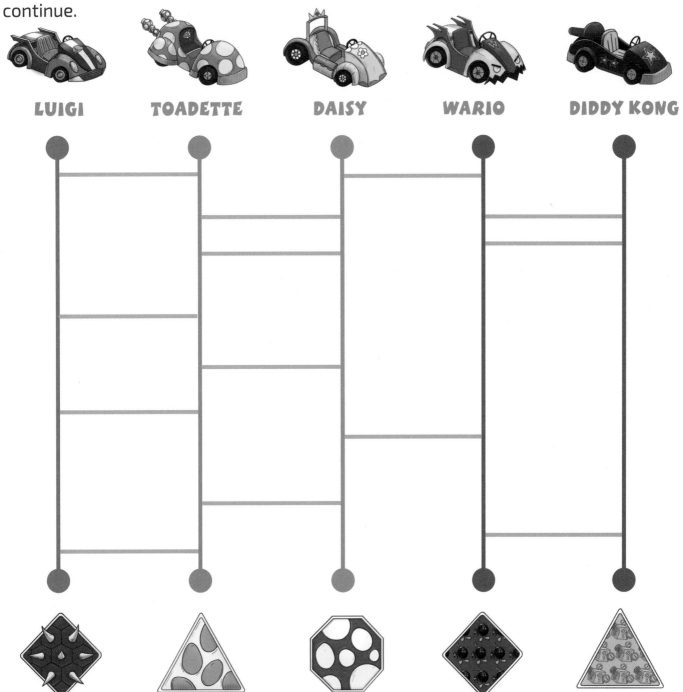

LUIGI **TOADETTE** **DAISY** **WARIO** **DIDDY KONG**

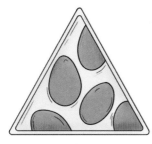

WORD LADDER

Can you transform the word "CAPE" into "DINO" in just 12 steps, changing only one letter each time? Answer the clues, and you'll get to the finish line.

CAPE

_____	1. Walking aid
_____	2. A short street
_____	3. Frappe Snow _____
_____	4. They back up Pauline
_____	5. Batman villain
_____	6. Lion hair
_____	7. Not yours
_____	8. Fork part
_____	9. _____ Trial
_____	10. Ten cents
_____	11. Eat

DINO

TIP

Receiving a driver you already have from a pipe pull isn't useless — duplicate characters combine to increase a skill level.

A VERY SPECIAL WORD SEARCH

In the puzzle below, find the words associated with the special tours and races in *Mario Kart Tour*.

Hammer Bro

Baby Rosaline

Valentines

Ice Tour

Holiday

Winter

Halloween

Spotlight

Kimono

Holiday Cheer

Reindeer

BusDriver

Wintertime

Vacation

Cherub

```
E W I N T E R T I M E U F J K U N S M N
W N O M D S O W Z P C X K C M H O T O T
R I I U L D H R E V I R D S U B I L Q H
M E N L R I A M Q L P F C C G D T H Y E
T E E T A R L B Y D K H M S G B A J N T
Y W Y D E S L T F M E Y P I X I C B K P
H O N W N R O Z I R S O B J T A A L O K
T A P D Q I W R U M T M S Q M V R Q K
Q I M Y B E E B Y L Y H P I S E O J N V
K N H M H E E R I B S C R F V E Z S H B
F J I A E C N G N E A U V X O H J Y U K
N S C T S R H Q N Z O B O B J C X S D V
S Y T K W T B I H T T L S V A Y E K K N
V L T G M F T R E L H O L I D A Y I J B
B K E O U N R C O B E Q G G Y D K M H R
L Y P D E B I C H Q D Q V D Q I I O D E
A V A L N E D B W X S I G K U L U N D C
U Q A I U F Z Q Y O X H E Q O O Z O H A
S V V C X K A Y B W E H C T M H J A S P
K A V J X H V A G Q D O M P K K K P C H
```

WHAT KART IS THAT?

Unscramble the names of the following karts in *Mario Kart Tour*.
The highlighted letters will spell out the name of a very special kart.

1. OAPKO HEDARS

☐☐☐☐☐ ☐☐☐☐☐☐☐

2. DASO EJT

☐☐☐☐ ☐☐☐

3. OYWLEL XITA

☐☐☐☐☐ ☐☐☐☐

4. TELLBU ARSHEB

☐☐☐☐☐☐ ☐☐☐☐☐☐

5. LMFEA LREFY

☐☐☐☐☐ ☐☐☐☐☐

6. RYHIBATD RILG

☐☐☐☐☐☐☐☐ ☐☐☐☐

7. URSPE OELPRBO

☐☐☐☐☐ ☐☐☐☐☐☐☐

8. IPPE MAREF

☐☐☐☐ ☐☐☐☐☐

9. ELBU BWNOGADA

☐☐☐☐ ☐☐☐☐☐☐☐☐

10. BUROT SOHIY

☐☐☐☐☐ ☐☐☐☐☐

ANSWER

54

____ ____ ____ ____ ____ ____ ____ ____ ____ ____

A NEW YORK MINUTE MAZE

It's a race through New York! Which entrance will get you to the finish line?

GUESS WHO?

With the clues below, figure out which racer we're talking about . . . or not talking about, as the case may be.

1. I wear a red hat, but I'm not a Mario of any type.

   _____

2. I'm a mushroom, but I'm not Toadette.

   _____

3. I'm a monkey, but I don't wear a tie.

   _____

4. I'm a tall lady, but I'm not royalty.

   _____

5. I've got a mustache, and I'm evil, but my name doesn't rhyme with another character's.

   _____

6. I'm a shiny Mario, but I'm far from "metal."

   _____

7. I'm a king, but I'm no reptile.

   _____

8. I'm a Koopa Kid, but I don't have any sisters.

   _____

IT'S YOUR STORY!

Write your own *Mario Kart Tour* racing story. Include at least four of the karts below to add detail to your adventure.

BOWSER	DIDDY KONG	DONKEY KONG	KOOPA TROOPA	LUIGI
DAISY	PRINCESS PEACH	TOADETTE	WARIO	MARIO

_____

_____

_____

_____

_____

_____

_____

_____

_____

_____

_____

_____

_____

ANSWERS

CORE CAST CROSSWORD P2

ACROSS
6. Luigi
7. Dry Bones
9. Daisy
11. Wario
12. Toad
14. Yoshi
15. Koopa Troopa

DOWN
1. Pauline
2. Waluigi
3. Birdo
4. Toadette
5. Peach
8. Rosalina
10. Mario
13. Bowser

NOT THE RIGHT KART P3

Kart number 3

PLACE THE PLACEMENTS P4

1. Mario
2. Wario
3. Donkey Kong
4. Daisy
5. Luigi
6. Koopa Troopa
7. Bowser
8. Toadette

A RACE AROUND THE BLOCKS P5

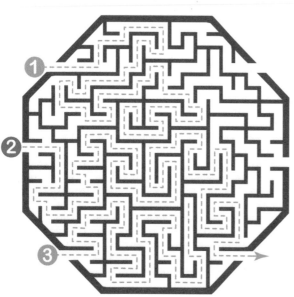

KART SEARCH P6

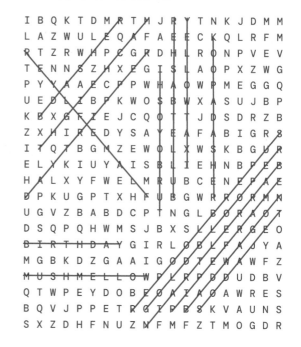

CONNECT THE DOTS: LOOKS GOOD P7

LUCKY HIDDEN WORD P8

1. Banana
2. Green Shell
3. Bob-omb
4. Mushroom
5. Super Horn
6. Lucky Seven
7. Red Shell

Revealed word: Blooper

SQUARED UP: ITEMS BY PICTURE P9

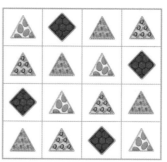

58

RACE TO THE BOTTOM P10

Mario — Third Place
Luigi — First Place
Princess — Fourth Place
Toadette — Second Place

FIND THE LUCKY 7 P11

The block with the lucky 7 in it is number 4.

BIG BEN, LITTLE DIFFERENCES P12

WORDS ARE FALLING P13

"Every character in *Mario Kart Tour* has to be unlocked."

BEFORE, AFTER, AND IN-BETWEEN P14

1. Ready, Set, Rocket Start
2. Big Reverse Race
3. Smash Small Dry Bones

COVERING YOUR TRACKS P15

ACROSS

3. Dino Dino Jungle
4. Rainbow Road
6. Mario Circuit
9. Shy Guy Bazaar
11. Daisy Hills
12. Waluigi Pinball
13. Luigi's Mansion
14. Choco Island

DOWN

1. Kalimari Desert
2. Toad Circuit
5. Koopa Troopa Beach
7. DK Pass
8. Cheep Cheep Lagoon
10. Rock Rock Mountain

FIND THE DIFFERENT DRIVERS P16

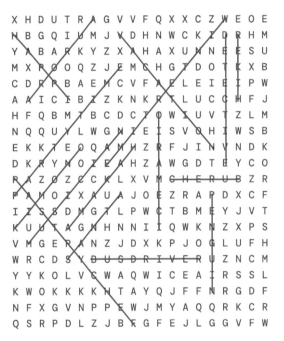

THE RACE IS ON! P17

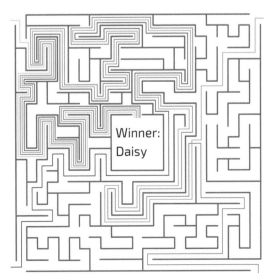

Winner: Daisy

JUST TWO WORDS P18

1. Wario
2. Air Balloon
3. Lakitu
4. Ultra-Mini Turbo
5. Iggy
6. Goomba
7. Ice Flower
8. Pauline
9. Item Ticket
10. Neo Bowser City
11. Baby Peach
12. Apple Kart
13. Landship
14. London Loop

Words spell out: Waluigi Pinball

READ AROUND P19

"Every race gives experience points."

PICTURE CROSSWORD P20

ACROSS

6. Ticket
8. Star
10. Triple Mushroom
11. Pipes

DOWN

1. Parachute
2. Hammer
3. Rubies
4. Boomerang
5. Coins
6. Tires
7. Kart
9. Spiny Shell

UNSCRAMBLE IT! P21

1. Shy Guy
2. Lakitu
3. Yoshi
4. Ludwig
5. Dry Bones
6. Roy

Highlighted letters spell: Glider

CONNECT THE DOTS: FIRE AWAY!

P22

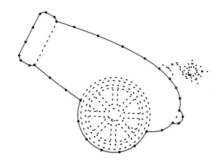

SQUARED UP: KOOPALINGS P24

R	E	W	I	Y	G	D	M	B
D	I	Y	E	M	B	W	R	G
M	B	G	R	D	W	Y	E	I
G	R	M	B	W	E	I	D	Y
I	D	B	M	G	Y	R	W	E
Y	W	E	D	R	I	G	B	M
B	M	D	G	I	R	E	Y	W
E	Y	I	W	B	D	M	G	R
W	G	R	Y	E	M	B	I	D

SPELLING TEST P25

1. Z (Bowser)
2. U (Vancouver)
3. C (Mushmellow)
4. C (Kalimari Desert)
5. H (Swooper)
6. I (Droplet)
7. N (Morton)
8. I (Dasher II)

Letters spell out: Zucchini

FIND THAT BONUS P26

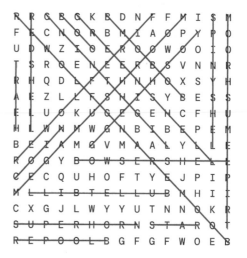

READ AROUND P27

"Keep your finger on the phone to drift."

SAME LETTER CONNECTOR P28

"You can get a special skill or item from a box."

REARRANGE AND ADD P29

Daisy — Dismay
Peach — Chapel
Wendy — Yawned

Roy — Rosy
Larry — Rarely
Morton — Monitor

Extra letters: M, L, A, S, E, I
Unscrambled: A SMILE

A RACE FOR THREE P30

HAZARDS CROSSWORD P31

ACROSS

5. Snake Jar
6. Noshi
7. Flipper
8. Thwomp
11. Swoop
12. Geyser
13. Lava Bubble
14. Bumper
15. Crate

DOWN

1. Barrel
2. Goat
3. Train
4. Clampy
5. Sidestepper
9. Oil Slick
10. Puddle
12. Goomba

REAL OR FAKE TRACKS? P32

REAL

New York Minute
Vancouver
 Velocity
Choco Island
Ghost Valley
Vanilla Lake
Waluigi Pinball
Frappe Snowland

Daisy Hills
Rock Rock
 Mountain
Dino Dino Jungle

FAKE

Hollywood
 Shuffle
Toronto Turnpike

Cake Mountain
Spooky Plains
Strawberry
 Island
Wario Foosball
Dessert Desert
Happy Village
Kong Kong Island
Boo Gardens

A PUZZLE TO FLY THROUGH P33

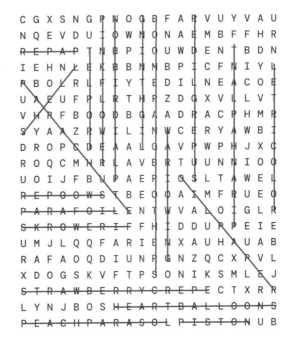

SQUARED UP: ITEMS BY PICTURE P34

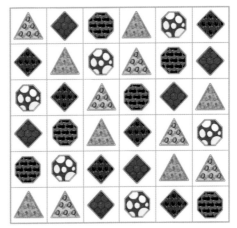

TOWER OF POWER P35

Towers number 3 and 7 are the same.

SO MANY MARIOS P36

1. Metal
2. Ice
3. Musician
4. Hakama
5. Santa
6. Gold
7. Classic
8. Happi
9. Baby

Phrase: It's a me, Mario

PLACE THE PLACEMENTS P37

1. Peach
2. Larry
3. King Boo
4. Pauline
5. Dry Bones
6. Toad
7. Ludwig
8. Shy Guy

READ AROUND P38

"You can use rubies to fire a pipe."

WORD LADDER P39

1. Road
2. Roar
3. Boar
4. Boat
5. Bart

TAKE ON KONG! P40

WORDS ARE FALLING P41

"Every racer, kart, and glider, can be leveled up."

DRIVEN OUT OF THE REAL WORLD

P42

ACROSS
1. Paris
3. Beach
6. New York
8. Mansion
9. City
11. Hills
12. London
13. Jungle

DOWN
1. Pinball
2. Lagoon
4. Tokyo
5. Mountain
7. Vancouver
10. Island

FUN-NAMED KART WORD SEARCH P43

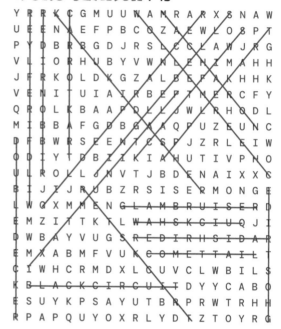

JUST TWO WORDS P44

1. Koopa Troopa
2. Ice Flower
3. New York
4. Gold Mario
5. Bowser
6. Oilpaper
7. Off-Road

Word spelled out: King Boo

WORD LADDER P45

1. Part
2. Past
3. Pass
4. Bass
5. Boss
6. Boot
7. Foot
8. Fort
9. Fore

SQUARED UP: TOUR STOPS P46

N	P	H	L	M	T	W	I	V
W	I	T	N	V	H	P	L	M
V	L	M	P	W	I	N	H	T
I	W	L	M	P	V	H	T	N
T	V	N	H	I	W	L	M	P
H	M	P	T	L	N	I	V	W
M	H	W	V	N	L	T	P	I

BEFORE, AFTER, AND IN-BETWEEN P

1. Goomba Takedown
2. Glider Challenge
3. Steer Clear of Obstacles

READ AROUND P48

"Clearing a daily challenge wins a grand star."

MARIO MATH P49

1. 6, because 5 would bring 495 coins, which isn't quite enough.
2. 10
3. 8
4. 32,000
5. The first option: 2,400 coins, vs. 2,200 coins.
6. 9,300
7. 3 super drivers, and you wouldn't have enough left for any quick tickets

ITEM RACE P51

Wario Kart — Mushroom
Toadette Kart — Bomb
Princess Daisy Kart — Coin block
Wario Kart — Yoshi egg
Diddy Kong Kart — Blue shell

CONNECT THE DOTS: FLOATING FRENZY P50

Latiku's cloud.

WORD LADDER P52

1. Cane
2. Lane
3. Land
4. Band
5. Bane
6. Mane
7. Mine
8. Tine
9. Time
10. Dime
11. Dine

A VERY SPECIAL WORD SEARCH P53

WHAT KART IS THAT? P54

1. Koopa Dasher
2. Soda Jet
3. Yellow Taxi
4. Bullet Basher
5. Flame Flyer
6. Birthday Girl
7. Super Blooper
8. Pipe Frame
9. Blue Badwagon
10. Turbo Yoshi

Revealed word: Daytripper

A NEW YORK MINUTE MAZE P55

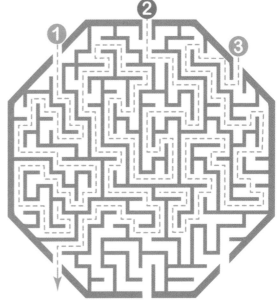

GUESS WHO? P56

1. Red Koopa
2. Toad
3. Diddy Kong
4. Pauline
5. Walugi
6. Gold Mario
7. King Boo
8. Wendy

Sky Pony Press books may be purchased in bulk at special discounts for sales promotion, corporate gifts, fund-raising, or educational purposes. Special editions can also be created to specifications. For details, contact the Special Sales Department, Sky Pony Press, 307 West 36th Street, 11th Floor, New York, NY 10018 or info@skyhorsepublishing.com.

Sky Pony® is a registered trademark of Skyhorse Publishing, Inc.®, a Delaware corporation.

Mario Kart® and Mario Kart Tour® are registered trademarks of Nintendo. The Mario Kart Tour game is copyright © Nintendo.

Visit our website at www.skyponypress.com.

10 9 8 7 6 5 4 3 2 1

Library of Congress Cataloging-in-Publication Data is available on file.

Cover design by Brian Peterson
Cover and interior artwork by Amanda Brack

Print ISBN: 978-1-5107-6305-0

Printed in China